20 Answers

∾

The Bible

Trent Horn

20 Answers: The Bible

Trent Horn

© 2016 Catholic Answers

Published by Catholic Answers, Inc.
2020 Gillespie Way
El Cajon, California 92020
1-888-291-8000 orders
619-387-0042 fax
catholic.com

Printed in the United States of America

978-1-68357-011-0
978-1-68357-012-7 Kindle
978-1-68357-013-4 ePub

Patrick

I thought as you [were] reading the bible — this little book may be of some interest to you. Love Pop

P.S. I've just done something toward your bible as [I'm] speaking & that's to write the Gospels. I've just completed — Matthew — Mark and Luke & am in the middle of Acts before a [burton] John.

Introduction

The Bible is the best-selling book of all time, and almost everyone has a strong opinion about it. An atheist might view the Bible as a bunch of made-up myths about God and miracles. Most Protestant Christians, on the other hand, see an inspired, inerrant book that is the only authoritative source of Christian doctrine. Other people think it has some nice stories and moral teachings, but don't consider it the word of God.

A Catholic approach to Scripture, in contrast, affirms that the Bible is inspired by God, but denies that it is the Christian's only rule of faith. It also affirms that the Bible, having God as its author, is without error. The words penned over a century ago by Pope Leo XIII, in defense of this controversial truth of the Faith, still resonate today:

> It is deplorable to see these attacks [on Scripture] growing every day more numerous and more severe. . . . By ridicule and scurrilous jesting, [critics] pervert the credulous and unformed minds of the young to the contempt of holy Scripture. . . . Should not these things, venerable brethren, stir up and set on fire the heart of every pastor, so that to this "knowledge, falsely so called," may be opposed the ancient and true science which the Church, through the apostles, has received from Christ, and that holy

Scripture may find the champions that are needed in so momentous a battle?[1]

This booklet has been written to help you become one of the champions of Scripture that Leo VIII called for. If that sounds daunting, don't worry: most of the objections that critics make against the Bible exhibit a few common patterns and cite only a small percentage of the Bible. By reviewing these patterns and commonly cited passages you can learn to defend Scripture without having to examine each of the Bible's approximately 35,000 individual verses.

Remember, though, that God has given us his word in Sacred Scripture, but the fullness of God's word is found only in his Son, Jesus Christ. That is because Christ is the Word incarnate (John 1:14) and he represents the one utterance in whom God expresses himself completely (CCC 102). Quoting the *Catechism of the Catholic Church*, Pope Benedict XVI wrote:

[T]he Christian faith is not a "religion of the book": Christianity is the "religion of the word of God," not of "a written and mute word, but of the incarnate and living Word." Consequently the Scripture is to be proclaimed, heard, read, received and experienced as the word of God, in the stream of the apostolic Tradition from which it is inseparable.[2]

1. What is the Bible?

The Bible (named from the Greek word for *book*) is a collection of books and letters, written over a period of centuries, that describe God's revelation to man and man's response to that revelation. The Bible, also called Sacred Scripture, is divided into two main parts: the Old Testament and the New Testament.

The first book of the Bible, Genesis, teaches that God created the world and made human beings in his image. It describes how our first parents rebelled against God and how God revealed himself to human beings in order to save them and their descendants from sin. This revelation took the form of *covenants,* such as those God made with Noah and Abraham, the latter of whom became the father of God's chosen people, Israel. God decreed that this group of people, named after Abraham's grandson Jacob, whom God later renamed Israel, would bless the entire world.

The next books of the Bible describe how Israel was enslaved in Egypt until God formed a covenant with Moses. Moses led Israel to freedom out of Egypt and into the desert, where they wandered for forty years before settling in a land God had promised to them in Canaan (located in modern-day Israel). The first five books of the Bible, which Jewish people call the Torah and scholars call the Pentateuch, end with the death of Moses and the installation of his successor, Joshua.

The books of Joshua and Judges continue Israel's story and describe how Israel contended with the hostile tribes that inhabited the land of Canaan.

Along with books that tell the story of God's people, the Old Testament (or Hebrew Bible) contains literature that teaches God's people wisdom and right living (such as the book of Proverbs). It also contains collections of prayers and hymns, such as those found in the book of Psalms. Other books in the Old Testament include stories that were written to teach people to have faith in God, such as the story of Job, who kept his faith in spite of tremendous suffering.

The remaining historical books of the Old Testament, for example, Samuel and Kings, describe how Israel became a nation, and then a kingdom, and then a divided kingdom. The most famous of Israel's kings was David, whom most people remember as the shepherd boy who defeated the Philistine giant Goliath with a sling and a stone. David's son Solomon succeeded, him but his inability to keep God's people from falling into idolatry and wickedness led to the nation being divided into northern and southern kingdoms.

After this division, God sent a series of prophets to exhort his people to repentance, but these prophetic reforms were either ignored or did not last. Not long after, other nations conquered both kingdoms and took God's people into captivity. The final historical books of the Old Testament reveal how God's people were freed from captivity and returned to their promised land. Unfortunately, even after their return God's people suffered under the rule of foreign powers such as the Greeks (and later the Romans). In response to this, they patiently awaited the Messiah: a savior promised in Scripture who would restore God's kingdom.

The New Testament is the story of that Messiah, Jesus Christ. The four Gospels (Matthew, Mark, Luke, and John) tell us that Jesus existed as the Son of God before the creation of the world and that he became man in order to save humanity from its sins. The Gospels describe how Jesus gathered twelve disciples, taught, healed, performed miracles, and died on a cross to atone for the world's sins. The Gospels end with an account of Christ's resurrection from the dead and his commissioning of the disciples to become apostles (a Greek word that means *messenger*) who would share this good news throughout the world.

The Acts of the Apostles is the book that picks up where the Gospels leave off (its author also wrote the Gospel of Luke) and describes how Christ's Church flourished in spite of the persecution it faced from Jewish and Roman leaders. The remainder of the New Testament includes a collection of letters the apostles sent to various communities in order to teach and encourage them to keep the Faith. The majority of these letters were written by St. Paul, a Jewish leader who persecuted the Church until he encountered the risen Christ and became a Christian.

The last book of the Bible is Revelation, which contains visions of God's heavenly kingdom given to the apostle John. It also contains prophecies about the end of the world and descriptions of how God will conquer evil and gather his people, both the living and the dead, unto himself in order to share glorious, eternal life with them.

2. How is the Bible the word of God?

When Christians say the Bible is inspired, or that it is the word of God, that phrase can be misunderstood. Some people think that calling the Bible the "word of God" means God himself penned every word in it and used some kind of heavenly parcel delivery service to send it down to earth. But Jews and Christians have always known that the parts of the Bible that came directly from God, such as the Ten Commandments that God wrote on the tablets at Mount Sinai, are few and far between. Instead, it was human beings who wrote the Bible's original manuscripts.

A more common mistake is to believe that although human beings wrote the physical words found in the Bible, they were only the *mechanical* authors of Scripture. According to this view, none of the Bible's texts came from the human authors' minds, but from God's mind alone. The human authors either recorded the revelation God dictated to them, or God took control of their bodies and wrote his revelation through them. As Protestant author Jasper James Ray put it, "The very words of the Bible were given to the authors, and not just the ideas they convey. The writers were not left to choose the words."[3]

The idea that the human authors of Scripture recorded what God said just as a stenographer records courtroom testimony is common in certain kinds of biblical fundamentalism, which, according to the Church's Pontifical Biblical Commission, "seeks to escape any closeness of the divine and the human . . . for this reason, it tends to treat the biblical text as if it had been dictated word for word by the Spirit. It fails to recognize that the word of God has been formulated in language and expression conditioned by various periods."[4]

This "dictation theory" of inspiration also doesn't make sense of passages such as 1 Corinthians 1:14–16, in which Paul wrote, "I am thankful that I baptized none of you except Crispus and Gaius; lest any one should say that you were baptized in my name. (I did baptize also the household of Stephanas. Beyond that, I do not know whether I baptized anyone else.)" Here Paul clearly didn't write down whatever God told him because God would have known who Paul baptized. Instead, Paul used his own ideas and own words to write to the Christians in Corinth.

That being said, God is still the author of Scripture even if the Bible's human authors used their own words and ideas when they wrote the Bible. According to the Second Vatican Council's document *Dei Verbum*:

> The books of both the Old and New Testaments in their entirety, with all their parts, are sacred and canonical because written under the inspiration of the Holy Spirit, they have God as their author and have been handed on as such to the Church herself. In composing the sacred books, God chose men and while employed by him they made use of their powers and abilities, so that with him acting in them and through them, they, as true authors, consigned to writing everything and only those things which he wanted.[5]

Another way to understand the inspiration of Scripture is to compare it to the Incarnation. Just as Christ is God's Word that became flesh and dwelt among us (John 1:14), Scripture is God's word made into written characters that dwells among us. *Dei Verbum* taught: "For the words of God, expressed in human language, have been made like human discourse, just as the word of the eternal Father, when he took to himself the flesh of human weakness, was in every way made like men."[6]

Pope St. John Paul II agreed and said in an address to the Pontifical Biblical Commission, "After the heavenly glorification of the humanity of the Word made flesh, it is again due to written words that his stay among us is attested to in an abiding way."[7]

Just as Christ's human nature did not contradict his divinity, the human words of Scripture do not contradict God's authorship of it, even though their finite nature limits what God can communicate through them. (This is unavoidable, because *any* way an infinite being chose to reveal himself to finite creatures would involve some limiting of the divine.) For instance, God allowed the human authors of Scripture to retain their own way of speaking about the natural world, even where that way of speaking does not correspond to our modern, scientific way of understanding it.

3. How should Catholics interpret Scripture?

The *Catechism of the Catholic Church* (CCC) tells us that there are two different senses of Scripture: the *literal* sense conveyed by the words of Scripture and the *spiritual* sense conveyed by the realities and events within those words (CCC 115–118). If we don't understand both senses we risk misunderstanding the sacred author's meaning.

Take Matthew 2:15's assertion that the infant Jesus' departure from Egypt fulfilled Hosea 11:1's prophecy, in which God says, "out of Egypt have I called my Son." This prophecy is literally about Israel, and Matthew knows this, but it was also spiritually fulfilled in Jesus. Matthew shows us that God, in his providence, used the Exodus as a "type" or "precursor" to model his future call, which brought his only-begotten Son out of Egypt and into Nazareth as an infant. In other words, the literal sense of Scripture recognizes how humans use *language* to communicate what they mean, whereas the symbolic sense recognizes how God, in his all-powerful and all-knowing providence, can use *events* in history to communicate what he means.

The Church also makes a crucial distinction between what is *written* in Scripture and what is *asserted* in Scripture. According to *Dei Verbum*, "everything asserted by the inspired authors or sacred writers must be held to be asserted by the Holy Spirit."[8] If I say, "It's raining cats and dogs outside" or "I have a million things to do today," the average listener will know that I am asserting a message that differs from what my words literally mean.

Of course, although it may be easy for modern English speakers to understand a fellow English speaker's assertions, understanding statements originally made in other languages and translated into one's own language becomes more difficult. This is especially true regarding the ancient cultural contexts in which the Bible was written. Pope Pius XII recognized this difficulty in 1943 when he wrote in the encyclical *Divino Afflante Spiritu*:

What is the literal sense of a passage is not always as obvious in the speeches and writings of the ancient authors of the East, as it is in the works of our own time. For what they wished to express is not to be determined by the rules of grammar and philology alone, nor solely by the context; the interpreter must, as it were, go back wholly in spirit to those remote centuries of the East and with the aid of history, archaeology, ethnology, and other sciences, accurately determine what modes of writing, so to speak, the authors of that ancient period would be likely to use, and in fact did use.[9]

That's why it is helpful to examine the *genre* of the biblical text in question—the literary category to which it belongs. As the Pontifical Biblical Commission notes, "In the Bible, we find different literary genres in use in that cultural area: poetry, prophecy, narrative, eschatological sayings, parables, hymns, confessions of faith, etc., each of which has its own way of presenting the truth."[10]

Another principle of interpreting Scripture is "the analogy of faith," or the idea that Scripture ought to be read against the whole of divine revelation (CCC 114). According to *Dei Verbum*: "[S]erious attention must be given to the content and unity of the whole of Scripture if the meaning of the sacred texts is to be correctly worked out. The living tradition of the whole Church must be taken into account along with the harmony which exists between elements of the faith."[11] Indeed, 2 Peter 1:20 says that "no prophecy of Scripture is a matter of one's own interpretation," and the author later warns his readers that some passages in the Bible are "hard to understand, which the ignorant and unstable twist to their own destruction" (2 Pet. 3:16).

Fortunately, Christ did not leave us as orphans (John 14:18). Instead, he gave us his Church guided by the Holy Spirit to be an infallible teacher on the nature and meaning of Sacred Scripture. That is why St. Paul called the Church "the pillar and foundation of truth" (1 Tim. 3:15) and the Second Vatican Council said, "The task of authentically interpreting the word of God, whether written or handed on, has been entrusted exclusively to the living teaching office of the Church, whose authority is exercised in the name of Jesus Christ."[12]

4. Why don't Catholics rely on the Bible alone?

Imagine if every American had the authority to decide what the U.S. Constitution means. Each person could do as he wished, claiming that his actions fell under his own interpretation of the words in the Constitution. What would come of this approach? Anarchy. Fortunately, America's Founding Fathers created the Supreme Court to interpret the Constitution.

Although the Supreme Court isn't divinely protected from error, as is the Church's Magisterium, through the Court's decisions a uniform legal code that bound all citizens equally would be ensured.

The Protestant Reformers believed that all the truth about Christianity comes from the Bible alone; or that the Bible is our sole, infallible rule of faith. They called this principle *sola scriptura* or "Scripture alone," but we might call it a "blueprint for anarchy."[13] Indeed, today we witness the proliferation of Protestant denominations that teach mutually contradictory positions on many important matters of faith. For just as personal interpretation of the Constitution would lead to chaos for the rule of law, relying solely on one's personal interpretation of the Bible as a guide to Christian doctrine leads to chaos for the rule of faith.

Interestingly, the Bible itself never asserts that all of divine revelation is found explicitly and only within its pages. It's true that Revelation 22:18 warns, "every one who hears the words of the prophecy of this book: if any one adds to them, God will add to him the plagues described in this book." But John, the author of Revelation, was just prohibiting the addition of words to the visions he received. He was not denying that the word of God exists outside of his own revelation (including the word found in other books of the Bible); neither could he have been referring to the Bible that would be assembled with his book at the end, hundreds of years later.

Another verse that is cited in defense of *sola scriptura* is Acts 17:11, which describes how the Jews in Berea "were more noble than those in Thessalonica, for they received the word with all eagerness, examining the scriptures daily to see if [Paul's teaching was true]." However, the Jews in Thessalonica were not ignorant of Scripture. They just opposed Paul's interpretation of Scripture because he "reasoned" and "proved" from it that Jesus was the Messiah. The Bereans, on the other hand, were more "noble" because they were open-minded and saw that Scripture was a witness to Paul's preaching. Luke even acknowledges that "the word of God had now been proclaimed by Paul in Berea" (Acts 17:13), which means that the word of God is not confined to written words alone.

However, the passage Protestants usually cite in favor of *sola scriptura* is 2 Timothy 3:16–17. In this letter, Paul tells his disciple Timothy how he should behave and grow as a man of God and leader in the Church. He writes, "All Scripture is inspired by God and profitable for teaching, for reproof, for correction, and for training in righteousness, that the man of God may be complete, equipped for every good work."

Of course, Catholics agree that all Scripture is inspired by God and is useful for teaching and training, but this doesn't mean that Scripture is the *only* thing that is useful in this way. Neither does it mean that Scripture is the only source of God's saving revelation. Some Protestants argue that this verse does say that Scripture alone is sufficient for salvation because it makes the man of God "equipped for every good work." But elsewhere Paul describes other things being able to make a man equipped to do "every good work," things that are not a Christian's sole source of doctrine. For example, in 2 Timothy 2:21 Paul says that if Timothy cleanses himself from bad influences he will be a vessel ready for "every good work," but that doesn't mean Timothy's prudence will cause him to know all the essential doctrines of the Faith.

In addition, if "every good work" refers to all essential doctrines, then how could Scripture equip the man of God to know what is and is not Scripture? After all, the Bible does not have an inspired table of contents (see answer 6). Instead, as the *Catechism* says: "the Church, to whom the transmission and interpretation of revelation is entrusted, does not derive her certainty about all revealed truths from the holy scriptures alone. Both Scripture and Tradition must be accepted and honored with equal sentiments of devotion and reverence" (CCC 82).

5. What is the relationship between Scripture and Tradition?

After Jesus' resurrection he commissioned the apostles to "make disciples of all nations" (Matt. 28:19) and be his witnesses "in Jerusalem and in all Judea and Samaria and to the end of the earth" (Acts 1:8). But prior to his ascension into heaven Jesus never commanded the apostles to write anything down. Instead, their mission was to preach the gospel. Paul even thanked the Thessalonians for accepting his preaching, not as human words, but as the very words of God (1 Thess. 2:13).

Remember, the first Christians didn't learn their faith from the Bible because the Bible didn't exist. None of the books of the New Testament had been written yet. During this time the word of God was transmitted orally, from Jesus to the apostles and their disciples, through what is called Sacred Tradition. Paul refers to it when he commends the Corinthians for "maintain[ing] the traditions even as I have delivered them to you" (1 Cor. 11:2) and instructs his disciple Timothy, "what you have heard from me before many witnesses entrust to faithful men who will be able to teach others also" (2 Tim. 2:2).

Eventually some of this oral proclamation of God's word was recorded and became Scripture, but even after that happened, God's word in Tradition remained. When Paul tells the Christians in the Greek city of Thessalonica to "stand firm and hold to the traditions which you were taught by us, either by word of mouth or by letter" (2 Thess. 2:15), he is exhorting them to obey God's word in both its forms. So Scripture and Tradition are not competitors but, as the *Catechism* says, are

"bound closely together, and communicate one with the other. For both of them, flowing out from the same divine well-spring, come together in some fashion to form one thing, and move towards the same goal." Each of them makes present and fruitful in the Church the mystery of Christ, who promised to remain with his own "always, to the close of the age" (CCC 80).

It's important to remember that Sacred Tradition is not the same as the customs and practices associated with the Church that can change over time (for example, manners of dress, styles of liturgy, etc.). The *Catechism* says, "The Tradition here in question comes from the apostles and hands on what they received from Jesus' teaching and example and what they learned from the Holy Spirit" (CCC 83). Tradition (with a capital "T") refers to the word of God that is "handed on" or "delivered" and does not change even though our understanding of it may deepen and grow over time (just as our understanding of Scripture deepens and grows over time).

In the second century St. Irenaeus served as a witness to this handing on of Tradition (the word itself literally means something handed on) when he said that "while the languages of the world are diverse, nevertheless, the authority of the tradition is one and the same." He also rhetorically asked his readers, "What if the apostles had not in fact left writings to us? Would it not be necessary to follow the order of Tradition, which was handed down to those to whom they entrusted the churches?"[14]

Some Protestants object to the idea of Sacred Tradition because they believe Jesus condemned it. They refer to the time when Jesus told the Pharisees, "for the sake of your tradition, you have made void the word of God" (Matt 15:6). But in this case Jesus was condemning a particular man-made tradition that was contrary to a divine commandment. Specifically, he criticized the tradition of selfishly applying *korban*, or a sacrificial offering, in a way that allowed money to be given as a gift to the temple in lieu of supporting one's aged parents—a tradition that nullified the Fourth Commandment, honor your father and mother.

We also know that Jesus did not reject the notion of an authoritative religious tradition. In Mathew 23:2–3 he told his disciples to obey the Pharisees because they sat on something called "Moses' seat." This was not an actual chair but a term that referred to a Jewish tradition, not found in Scripture, about the Pharisees' teaching authority.

Catholics believe that the word of God cannot contradict itself, so if a tradition contradicts Scripture, then the tradition must be of human—small "t"— rather than divine—capital "T"— origin. Conversely, if a document purporting to be Scripture (such as a forged or heretical Gospel) contradicts Sacred Tradition or if someone's interpretation of Scripture contradicts it, then we know that it, too, is of human origin.

St. Vincent of Lerins made this point in the fifth century when he noticed that heretics could cite Scripture just as well as the faithful. This meant that another authority was necessary to arbitrate theological disputes. "It is very necessary," he wrote, "on account of so great intricacies of such various error, that the rule for the right understanding of the prophets and apostles should be framed in accordance with the standard of ecclesiastical and Catholic interpretation."[15]

6. How do we know which writings belong in the Bible?

The collection of books and letters considered to be part of Sacred Scripture is called the canon of Scripture. The word *canon* comes from a Greek word that means *rule*, and refers to the Church's official list of inspired writings. In contrast to the Catholic view of the canon, Protestants claim that an authoritative Church is not needed to determine which ancient writings are inspired. Some Protestants even say it's obvious which books belong in the Bible and which do not.

But is it really so obvious?

After all, some books of the Bible don't seem very "biblical." Ecclesiastes contains what seems to be a cynical rejection of the afterlife, the third letter of John doesn't even mention the name of Jesus Christ, and the letter to Philemon doesn't teach any specific doctrine.

The part of the book of Esther that Protestants consider to be inspired Scripture never even mentions God! Yet, all these writings are found in the Bible, although other writings that were popular in the early Church, such as the *Didache* or the letter of Clement (which was even read in early Church services) are not.[16]

Without an authoritative Church they can trust, how do Protestants know what's in the canon and what isn't? The Protestant theologian R.C. Sproul famously suggested that the best we can say is that the canon of Scripture is "a fallible list of infallible books."[17] It's fallible because, from Sproul's point of view, the Church that pronounced the canon had no real authority. But if a non-authoritative group of Christians in the third and fourth centuries could decide what the canon of Scripture was, then why couldn't another non-authoritative group of Christians do the same today?

For example, in 2013, Hal Taussig, a member of a group of skeptical scholars called the Jesus Seminar, published a collection called *A New New Testament.* Added to the traditional New Testament were second-century apocryphal gospels such as "The Gospel of Truth," as well as texts from the Dead Sea Scrolls like "The Thunder: Perfect Mind." Most Protestants would never accept such books as part of the Bible, but what authority do they have to say someone like Taussig is wrong?

After all, 500 years ago, Martin Luther and other reformers made their own tweaks to the canon. Luther called the letter of James "an epistle of straw" because it contradicted his theology of justification by faith alone (James 2:24 says, for example, that we are *not* justified by faith alone).[18] Although that letter remained in the Bible, Luther and the other Reformers did remove the deuterocanonical books (e.g., Sirach, Tobit, 1 and 2 Maccabees, and others) from the Old Testament, and they are still absent from Protestant bibles (see answer 7).[19] How can Protestants denounce Taussig's alteration of the canon without undermining the Reformers' decision to alter the canon in the sixteenth century?

Even some Protestants understand the difficulties that the canon poses for their theology. According to prominent Reformed theologian Douglas Wilson:

> The problem with contemporary Protestants is that they have no doctrine of the Table of Contents. With the approach that is popular in conservative evangelical circles, one simply comes to the Bible by means of an epistemological lurch. The Bible "just is," and any questions about how it got here are dismissed as a nuisance. But time passes, the questions remain unanswered, the silence becomes awkward, and conversions of thoughtful evangelicals to Rome proceed apace.[20]

If the Catholic Church has divine authority from Christ, however, then we don't have to say that the

Bible "just is." We can say that the Church has the power to recognize and pronounce the true canon of Scripture. This is in fact what happened. Pope Damasus first promulgated the canon at the synod in Rome (382), and it was later defined at the regional councils of Hippo (393) and Carthage (397). The Church reaffirmed the canon at the ecumenical council of Trent (1545–1563) after the Protestant Reformers challenged its inclusion of certain books (the *deuterocanonical* or "second canon" books) of Scripture.

The Church's authority to select the canon doesn't mean the Church has a higher authority than Scripture, but rather, as the Second Vatican Council taught, the Church

> serves [the word of God], teaching only what has been handed on, listening to it devoutly, guarding it scrupulously and explaining it faithfully in accord with a divine commission and with the help of the Holy Spirit, it draws from this one deposit of faith everything which it presents for belief as divinely revealed.[21]

7. Why are Catholic bibles bigger than Protestant bibles?

Protestant bibles have sixty-six books in them: twenty-seven in the New Testament and thirty-nine in the Old Testament. Catholic bibles have the same number of books in the New Testament, but they have six more books in the Old Testament (Tobit, Judith, Wisdom, Sirach, Baruch, and 1 and 2 Maccabees) as well as more chapters in the books of Esther and Daniel. Catholics refer to these books as deuterocanonical, whereas Protestants call them the "apocrypha" and consider them as uninspired as any other nonbiblical work.

Catholics bibles contain the deuterocanonicals because those books were part of the Bible that Jesus and the apostles used. Called the Septuagint, it was the Greek translation of the Old Testament and was widely used in the early Church due to the fact that Greek (like English today) was a universal language of commerce.

Some Protestants say we should not include the deuterocanonical books in the canon because Jesus and the apostles never quoted from them elsewhere in Scripture. But those aren't the only books that aren't quoted elsewhere. As Protestant scholar Bruce Metzger observes, "nowhere in the New Testament is there a direct quotation from the canonical books of Joshua, Judges, Chronicles, Ezra, Nehemiah, Esther, Ecclesiastes, the Song of Solomon, Obadiah, Zephaniah, and Nahum; and the New Testament allusions to them are few in number."[22]

In fact, the New Testament authors never even *allude* to Esther, Ecclesiastes, or the Song of Solomon despite the fact that the content of these books was relevant to their own writings. They did, however, allude to the deuterocanonical books, such as in Mark 12:18–22, where the Sadducees question Jesus about a woman who was married to seven brothers who all died consecutively. That story is from the deuterocanonical book of Tobit, yet Jesus doesn't dismiss it as apocryphal.

Another example is Hebrews 11:35, where the author mentions how some women "received their dead by resurrection. Some were tortured, refusing to accept release, that they might rise again to a better life." This refers to persecutions found in 2 Maccabees 7, where a group of brothers suffer martyrdom instead of violating God's law. Their mother said, "Do not fear this butcher, but prove worthy of your brothers. Accept death, so that in God's mercy I may get you back again with your brothers" (2 Macc. 7:29).

Finally, in Matthew 27:39–43 the crowd and the Jewish leaders taunt Jesus because he declared himself to be the son of God yet God didn't save him from being crucified. This passage is a clear allusion to the deuterocanonical book of Wisdom, which says, "if the righteous man is God's son, he will help him, and will deliver him from the hand of his adversaries" (2:18). The crowd's gloating that God had failed to do this for Jesus only makes sense if they believed the book of Wisdom was inspired in what it said about the Son of God.

Some Protestants say that at the end of the first century A.D. a Jewish gathering called the Council of Jamnia definitively established the Hebrew canon, and Christians should abide by that decision. But, aside from evidence that there actually was no Council of Jamnia,[23] this argument would justify rejecting the canonical Gospels, too, because they were also allegedly rejected at this council! It may even be the case that the Jews who did reject the deuterocanonical books did so because they had become popular with Christians, who in their eyes were just apostate Jews.[24]

So the real question is not, "Why are Catholic bibles bigger?" Rather it's, "Why are Protestant bibles smaller?" The deuterocanonical books were considered inspired Scripture for centuries until Protestant Reformers lsuch as Martin Luther jettisoned them because they taught doctrines that conflicted with their novel theology. (The most famous example would be 2 Maccabees 12:46, which teaches the efficacy of praying for the dead in order to atone for their sins.)

But the first Christians saw no problems with these teachings, as is evidenced in Church Fathers such as Clement of Rome, Irenaeus, Athenagoras, Clement of Alexandria, Origen, Methodius, Cyprian, Athanasius, and Augustine, who all cited the deuterocanonical books as Scripture.[25] As the Anglican scholar J.N.D. Kelly wrote, for the great majority of the early Church Fathers "the deuterocanonical writings ranked as Scripture in the fullest sense."[26]

8. What does it mean for Scripture to be inerrant?

Because the Bible is *inspired* (God is its author), it follows that the Bible must be *inerrant,* or free from error. This means that God prevented the human authors of Scripture from asserting something false in the original biblical texts. Allegations of error in Scripture cannot be explained away as the inevitable by-product of the Bible's human authors. As St. Basil the Great said in the fourth century, "What is the distinctive mark of faith? Full and unhesitating certainty that the words inspired by God are true."[27]

Since before Basil's time, the Church has uniformly taught that Scripture is without error. Pope Leo XIII wrote in his 1893 encyclical *Providentissimus Deus*:

[I]nspiration not only is essentially incompatible with error, but excludes and rejects it as absolutely and necessarily as it is impossible that God Himself, the supreme Truth, can utter that which is not true. This is the ancient and unchanging faith of the Church, solemnly defined in the Councils of Florence and of Trent, and finally confirmed and more expressly formulated by the Council of the Vatican.[28]

But what it means for the Bible to be inerrant is not as simple as that. Taken to an extreme, the claim that the Bible is without error would mean that the Bible could not possess any details that do not correspond to a modern, scientific worldview. The Pontifical Biblical Commission elaborates:

> [W]ith the progressive discoveries in the field of history, philology, and the natural sciences, and because of the application to biblical research of the historical-critical method, exegetes have had to recognize that not everything in the Bible is expressed in accordance with the demands of the contemporary sciences, because the biblical writers reflect the limits of their own personal knowledge, in addition to those of their time and culture. The Second Vatican Council had to confront this problem in the preparation of the dogmatic constitution *Dei Verbum*.[29]

There are a variety of genres in scripture, and none of them assert a scientific description of the natural world. That is why *Dei Verbum*, the Council's Dogmatic Constitution on Divine Revelation, does not teach that everything *written* in Scripture is without error. Instead, it teaches that:

> [S]ince everything *asserted* [emphasis added] by the inspired authors or sacred writers must be held to be asserted by the Holy Spirit, it follows that the books of Scripture must be acknowledged as

teaching solidly, faithfully and without error that truth which God wanted put into sacred writings for the sake of salvation.[30]

The last phrase, "for the sake of salvation," is debated among some theologians. The traditional view is that this phrase refers to God's *purpose* in putting inerrant truth into the sacred writings: that it was done for our salvation. Another school of thought holds that it refers to *which truths* in Scripture God protected from error; that Scripture's inerrancy is restricted only to those parts of it that are "for the sake of [our] salvation." Other statements in the Bible not related to our salvation, especially those concerning scientific and historical facts, could be in error. Although some Catholic theologians and scholars endorse this latter view, it is not the historic view of inerrancy, and there are good reasons to be skeptical of it.[31]

Nearly twenty years before the Second Vatican Council (1962–1965), Pope Pius XII condemned the actions of those who "ventured to restrict the truth of Sacred Scripture solely to matters of faith and morals," and also said that Pope Leo XIII had "justly and rightly condemned these errors" in *Providentissimus Deus*.[32] *Dei Verbum* says that the human authors of Scripture were "true authors, consigned to writing everything and *only those things which he* [God] *wanted* [emphasis added]."[33]

This statement applies not just to truths given to us for the sake of our salvation, but to everything written in the Bible. To say that the Bible contains errors is to say that God wanted to inscribe errors into the biblical text, which would contradict his perfection and undermine our ability to trust the revelation he gave us. Of course, saying the Bible is free from error does not mean there are not apparent errors or difficult texts whose explanation is not clear.

Working through parts of Scripture that may seem to contain error takes time and careful study. Although the Church has taught that certain conclusions about the Bible (for example, that it is not divinely inspired) are opposed to the Faith, it has not explained the meaning of every passage in Scripture. That is an ongoing effort for all the faithful. As Pope Benedict XVI said:

The correct interpretation of these [difficult] passages requires a degree of expertise, acquired through a training that interprets the texts in their historical-literary context and within the Christian perspective which has as its ultimate hermeneutical key "the gospel and the new commandment of Jesus Christ brought about in the paschal mystery." I encourage scholars and pastors to help all the faithful to approach these passages through an interpretation which enables their meaning to emerge in the light of the mystery of Christ.[34]

9. How can the Bible be inspired when the book of Genesis contradicts science?

According to "young-earth" creationists, the book of Genesis says that God created the world in six 24-hour days. According to the theory of evolution, life evolved over billions of years through a slow and gradual process.[35] Doesn't it follow then that Genesis contradicts modern biology?

You may be surprised to learn that long before Darwin's theory of evolution was published in 1859, critics of the Church attacked the creation account in Genesis. In the fourth century, for example, a group of heretics called the Manichees challenged the authority of Scripture by asking how day and night could have existed before the creation of the sun on the fourth day.[36] Indeed, any reader, ancient or modern, should be puzzled by the fact that Genesis 1:3 describes how God created "light" on the first day, but created the sun, the thing that makes the light, on the fourth day. How do we explain this odd sequence of events?

Imagine that you're trying to recount what happened on a recent family vacation. How would you tell the story? You could present it in *chronological* order and talk about the long drive to the beach, the mix-up checking into the hotel, the visit to Grandma, then lounging on the beach, getting lost downtown, and stopping at a cheesy tourist trap on the way home.

Or, you could present it in *topical* order. You could first tell someone about your favorite parts of the trip—going to the beach, seeing Grandma, stopping at the tourist trap. Then, you might follow this with a description of your least favorite parts of the trip—the boring drive, the mix-up at the hotel, and getting lost in an unfamiliar place. Both approaches would be valid ways of retelling the story, even though one of them, the topical method, seems inaccurate if the listener assumed you were telling the story in chronological order.

The early Church Fathers and ecclesial writers understood this distinction and responded to critics accordingly. St. Augustine told the Manichees that the fourth day of creation symbolically demonstrates how God gave the sun and moon authority to rule over the kingdoms created during the first three days. Augustine went on to say that he believed God created the world instantly: "The sacred writer was able to separate in the time of his narrative what God did not separate in time in his creative act."[37] He even proposed the idea that God could have planted within the universe "dormant seeds" that would grow and take different forms over time—not unlike the change that occurs in living species through the process of evolution.[38]

The Catholic Church teaches that the first eleven chapters of Genesis contain historical truths that answer these basic questions (that is, God created everything and made humans in his image so that they could know and adore him as the one, true God). But those chapters, in the words of Pope Pius XII, in "simple and metaphorical language adapted to the mentality of a people but little cultured, both state the principal truths which are fundamental for our salvation, and also give a popular description of the origin of the human race and the chosen people."[39]

Think about how a parent might explain to his child that babies "come from a seed daddies give to mommies that grow inside the mommy's tummy." That's a true explanation but it shouldn't be taken literally since it was accommodated for a child's level of understanding. Likewise, the stories in Genesis are true but consist of nonliteral language that comes down to the level of understanding found in the audience that first heard these stories. Pope St. John Paul II even referred to the creation stories in Genesis as "myths," but he was also adamant that they were not mere fictions:

[T]he language in question is a mythical one. In this case, the term "myth" does not designate a fabulous content, but merely an archaic way of expressing a deeper content. Without any difficulty we discover that content, under the layer of the ancient narrative. It is really marvelous as regards the qualities and the condensation of the truths contained in it.[40]

The *Catechism* says, "The account of the fall in Genesis 3 uses figurative language but affirms a primeval event, a deed that took place at the beginning of the history of man" (CCC 390). So, for example, Genesis 3's language about talking snakes and eating forbidden fruit may be a figurative way of describing our first parents' sin.

The Catholic Church has infallibly taught that God created the world from nothing by his own free choice and that he made man's immortal soul in his image.[41] The Church has not, however, taught about the precise method God used to create the world or how old it is. Since a Catholic is free to form his own opinion on those questions, the critic can't say that our faith asserts a scientifically inaccurate description of the world.

10. Hasn't modern archaeology disproved the historical events of the Bible?

Modern archaeology has actually helped substantiate many of the Bible's claims and continues to illuminate the meaning of Sacred Scripture. For example, consider a slab of granite called the Merneptah Stele that has been dated to 1208 B.C. It contains a text describing the Egyptian pharaoh Merneptah's victories in the region and includes this boast, "Israel is laid waste and his seed is not." Since ethnic groups are often named after people they came from, this stele provides early evidence for the existence of a person named Israel from whom the ethnic group "Israel" originated.[42]

It's important to remember, though, that only some of the books in the Old Testament are strictly historical in nature. Others are poetic and use fictional elements to communicate their message to the reader. These may include the story of Jonah being swallowed by a "great fish" or Job's endurance of suffering. Jesus really told a story about the prodigal son, but the son himself may never have existed. In one of his Wednesday audiences, Pope St. John Paul II described other Old Testament books that fit this genre: "The books of Tobit, Judith, and Esther, although dealing with the history of the chosen people, have the character of allegorical and moral narrative rather than history properly so called."[43]

Other objections to the historical books of the Bible try to make arguments from silence or lack of evidence. For example, some argue that the absence of sources or artifacts from the Exodus (the Israelites' escape from captivity in Egypt) shows that this biblical event never happened. Now, it's true these sources have not been discovered yet, and it's even possible that they no longer exist. One reason is that the Israelites settled in Goshen (Gen. 45:10), which lies in the eastern part of the Nile Delta. The annual flooding of the Nile into this region would have regularly covered areas with new topsoil, thus making artifacts and documents difficult or impossible to recover.

Israel Finkelstein, an archaeologist who is very skeptical of the historicity of the events described in the Old Testament, even admits, "Nomadic societies do not establish permanent houses, and the constant migration permits them to move only minimal belongings. Moreover, their limited resources do not facilitate the creation of a flourishing material culture that could leave rich archaeological finds."[44] In other words, just because nomads did not leave artifacts for us to find does not prove they never existed in the first place.

Finally, we must expose a hidden assumption in the critics' arguments. Some people will say, "Even if the accounts of the patriarchs, or the Exodus, or the Israelites in Canaan are consistent, that doesn't prove those accounts describe real events in history. They could just be pieces of historical fiction." But when people say this they are assuming that unless a historical event described in the Bible is also described in a nonbiblical work, then either the event never happened or we have no way of knowing if it did happen.

This way of approaching Scripture, what some call a "hermeneutic of suspicion," treats the historical accounts in the Bible as being "guilty until proven innocent." If a justification is given for this assumption, it's usually that the Bible describes miracles and that makes its historical accounts unreliable. But other ancient historians like Josephus, Tacitus, and Suetonius also record miracles and fantastic events, and their knowledge of the ancient world isn't deemed "suspect" without outside corroboration. In many cases these writers represent our sole historical source for particular historical episodes.

One last point to emphasize is that historical critics who rejected the Bible because it was the only witness to something and lacked archaeological corroboration have been proven wrong before. Prior to the late nineteenth century, the Bible was the only source that attested to the existence of the Hittites (Gen. 50:13, Deut. 20:17, 1 Sam. 26:5). Since no other works or artifacts corroborated their existence, modern critics said this was yet another example of the Bible getting ancient history wrong.[45]

But in 1880, an expert in Assyrian culture named Archibald Henry Sayce delivered a lecture in England demonstrating that hieroglyphics found in Turkey and Syria showed that the Hittites had indeed existed at one time. Then in the early twentieth century, thousands of stone tablets were discovered in that region, and after Bedřich Hrozný translated them in 1915 a new historical science called Hittitology, or the study of Hittite culture, was born.[46]

Because of the incomplete nature of the ancient historical record, it's not implausible that an event like the Exodus could have occurred with only the Israelites successfully passing on the story through their oral and written tradition. The fact that the Israelites in the Old Testament or Christians in the New were the sole witnesses to an event does not prove that it didn't happen.

11. How can you trust the Gospels as biographical accounts of Christ's life when they are just anonymous documents written long after the events they claim to describe?

Critics of the New Testament often claim that the names of the authors of the Gospels were added after they had already been in circulation in the Church. Instead of Matthew, Mark, Luke, and John, they say, the real authors were anonymous Christians who relied on hearsay and legend rather than eyewitness testimony. But is there evidence for this claim?

First, it should be noted that even if the earliest copies of the Gospels did not contain the names of their authors, that would not disprove the traditional authorship of those texts. The works of the ancient Roman historian Tacitus often do not bear his name, but very few historians have ever questioned that Tacitus wrote them. We know Tacitus is the author of these works because other ancient writers, such as St. Jerome, identify him as the author.[47]

St. Augustine dealt with the charge that the Gospels were anonymous in the fourth century in his reply to a heretic named Faustus:

How do we know the authorship of the works of Plato, Aristotle, Cicero, Varro, and other similar writers, but by the unbroken chain of evidence? So also with the numerous commentaries on the ecclesiastical books, which have no canonical authority, and yet show a desire of usefulness and a spirit of inquiry. . . . How can we be sure of the authorship of any book, if we doubt the apostolic origin of those books which are attributed to the apostles by the Church which the apostles themselves founded.[48]

Furthermore, there is no compelling evidence that the first manuscripts of the Gospels *did* lack attribution to their traditional authors. There are no manuscripts that simply lack titles (as lay critics might imagine), and academic critics say the variants in the titles of those early manuscripts prove the authors' names were added at a much later date.[49] However, the usual variant is just the absence of the word "Gospel," which leaves a title that begins with "According to . . ." followed by the author's name—a name that is never absent from these manuscripts. Biblical scholar Brant Pitre says, "According to the basic rules of textual criticism, then, if anything is original in the titles, it is the names of the authors. They are at least as original as any other part of the Gospels for which we have unanimous manuscript evidence."[50]

Another argument in favor of the traditional authorship of the Gospels is this: if they had indeed been forged, the forgers would certainly have pretended to be more impressive-sounding authors. This is what heretics in the second, third, and fourth centuries did when they attributed their forged Gospels to people such as Peter, Philip, and even Mary Magdalene. Why pretend to be a relative unknown like Mark or Luke? Why would they impersonate a former tax collector like Matthew whose popularity would have been only slightly higher than Judas Iscariot's?[51]

What about the argument that the Gospels were written at least forty years after the death of Christ, which would make it difficult if not impossible to accurately remember the events of his life? Granted, forty or fifty years is a long time but the events surrounding Jesus' life and ministry would have left an indelible mark on the apostles' memories. Their ability to remember the events of Jesus' life would be comparable to a veteran in the year 2016 remembering what he did during the Vietnam War.

We also have to remember that our "memory muscles" atrophy as a result of using electronic recording devices instead (such as when we fail to remember telephone numbers and rely on the directory in our phones instead). This was not the case in Jesus' time, and the Jewish Talmud even records how some rabbis could memorize the entire Old Testament.[52] In addition, Jesus was a traveling preacher who delivered the same sermons throughout his travels, many of which contain poetic structure or memorable puns. The apostles would have heard his teachings dozens if not hundreds of times and then repeated them in their own preaching, thus making the deeds and teachings of Christ easy to remember.

There is also evidence that the Gospels were written before A.D. 70 because the book of Acts, which critics say was authored in the mid-80s, does not mention the destruction of Jerusalem or the deaths of its main protagonists, Peter and Paul. One plausible explanation is that Luke, the author of Acts, did not record these events because they hadn't happened yet. That would place the composition of Acts in the early 60s and the Gospel of Luke even earlier. Mark and Matthew would have been written earlier still, since most scholars believe they predate Luke. This would result in the first Gospel being written just two decades after the death of Christ, which is remarkable given that other ancient biographies, such as those of Alexander the Great or the Buddha, were written centuries after the deaths of their subjects.[53]

12. What about the thousands of contradictions in the Bible? Don't they disprove the inerrancy of Scripture?

Have you ever heard someone tell you that there are hundreds, if not thousands, of alleged contradictions within the Bible's pages? Maybe they sent you to a website such as www.1001biblecontradictions.com? This kind of argument is nothing new, and even the early Church Fathers were concerned about harmonizing alleged contradictions raised by their pagan opponents. So how should believers respond to these allegations? First, there are some simple rules to remember when reading the Bible that can help you resolve many alleged contradictions:

- *Read it in context.* Sometimes biblical passages only sound contradictory because they are isolated from their original context. Find the context and you'll usually find the explanation of the passage.

- *Consult a reliable commentary.* Commentaries provide details or facts not found in Scripture that can help explain alleged contradictions.

- *Differing descriptions do not equal contradictions.* The authors of Scripture may have differed in their descriptions of an event's details, but not in the essential truths they were asserting about those events. Some of them may have also written in different styles (topical vs. chronological), which can explain alleged discrepancies between them.

- *Incomplete is not inaccurate.* Just because the sacred author did not record something another author recorded does not mean his text is in error.

- *Only the original texts are inspired, not their copies.* Errors that came about through the copying process do not fall under the doctrine of inerrancy and can usually be located and corrected with ease.

- *The burden of proof is on the critic, not the believer.* If a critic alleges that Scripture is in error, he has the burden of proving that is the case. If the believer even shows a *possible* way of resolving the text, then the critic's objection that there is an intractable contradiction is refuted.

Second, you can consult one of the large encyclopedias of Bible difficulties published by Christians who have addressed these issues in detail. Unfortunately, the majority of the authors of such works are non-Catholics, so some of their explanations may conflict with Catholic teaching. My book *Hard Sayings: A Catholic Approach to Answering Bible Difficulties* addresses dozens of these alleged contradictions from a Catholic perspective.

Finally, we should give God's word the benefit of the doubt. Even if we can't resolve a difficulty at the present moment, it doesn't mean that the Bible is in error or that it is uninspired. It just means *we* don't know how to resolve the difficulty in question. This attitude is seen in early Church Fathers such as Justin Martyr, who told critics in the second century, "[Since] I am entirely convinced that no scripture contradicts another, I shall admit rather that I do not understand what is recorded, and shall strive to persuade those who imagine that the scriptures are contradictory, to be rather of the same opinion as myself."[54]

Maybe someone else has already resolved a particular difficulty but we aren't aware of it, or perhaps an explanation will arise when additional evidence is discovered in the future. The bottom line is that the truth of what God has revealed to us does not depend on our ability to defend that revelation in discussions or debates with nonbelievers. The *Catechism* teaches: "Faith is certain. It is more certain than all human knowledge because it is founded on the very word of God who cannot lie. To be sure, revealed truths can seem obscure to human reason and experience, but 'the certainty that the divine light gives is greater than that which the light of natural reason gives'" (CCC 157).

Karl Keating offers a good attitude to have in the face of alleged contradictions:

If you think [the Bible] is supposed to be a listing of theological propositions, you won't make heads or tails of it. If you think it is written in literary forms you're most familiar with, you'll go astray in interpreting it. Your only safe bet is to read it with the mind of the Church, which affirms the Bible's inerrancy. If you do that, you'll see that it contains no fundamental contradictions because, being God's inspired word, it's wholly true and can't be anything else."[55]

13. The Old Testament is full of archaic laws. Do we have to follow them?

St. Paul taught that the Mosaic Law was useful in teaching the Jews how to be holy, but it was incapable of saving them from sin (Gal. 3:10). That's because no one could perfectly follow the Law and the Law didn't fix the root of why we sin—our fallen nature. The Law was holy, good, and just (Rom. 7:12), but it made nothing perfect (Heb. 7:19).[56] It contained what the Second Vatican Council calls "imperfect and provisional" things like animal sacrifices or ritual cleansing that would not be a part of God's final, universal plan to redeem all of humanity.[57]

Simply put, we are not saved by obeying the law of Moses, but by obeying the Law of Christ (Gal 6:2). We rely on his grace (Eph. 2:8–10) to purify us from sin (1 John 1:7) and make us God's adopted children (Rom. 8:15). It is only through grace that we are able to follow Jesus' command to be perfect "as your heavenly father is perfect" (Matt 5:48).

But, even though some of the Old Testament's laws are for this reason not binding on Christians, others are. The ceremonial laws of the Old Testament dealt with principles of purity that were only applicable to Jews living before the coming of Christ. The moral laws, however, dealt with principles of right and wrong that remained applicable even after the coming of Christ. According to Scripture professor Mark Giszczak, "Aquinas teaches that the ritual and judicial laws have been abrogated, but that the moral law still holds. So we *can* eat bacon, but we can't eat our neighbor."[58]

Here's an analogy to help us understand this distinction. When I was a child, my mom gave me two rules: hold her hand when I cross the street, and don't drink from the bottles under the sink. Today, I only have to follow the latter rule. The former rule is no longer needed to protect me; in fact, following it could do me more harm than good. But it's just as unhealthy for me to break the latter rule now as it was then.

The ritual/judicial laws were like mom's hand-holding rule. They helped the Israelites understand the internal purity God's law requires, just as hand-holding helped me understand the vigilance that crossing the street required. These laws also protected the Israelites from pagan influences, just as the hand-holding rule protected me from careless motorists. But by the time of the New Covenant, these laws were no longer needed. In fact, the burden of following some of them (such as the requirement to be circumcised) hindered the goal of bringing non-Jews into communion with God.

As a result, Christ's Church, endowed with his authority (Matt. 16:18, Luke 10:16), removed the necessity of following these laws (Acts 15:6–21).[59] Through the coming of Christ, we have been discharged from following the entire Mosaic Law (Rom. 7:6), and Jesus himself "declared all foods clean" (Mark 7:19). The *Catechism* says, "Jesus perfects the dietary law, so important in Jewish daily life, by revealing its pedagogical meaning through a divine interpretation . . . 'What comes out of a man is what defiles a man. For from within, out of the heart of man, come evil thoughts'" (CCC 582).

However, unlike its ritual or temporary judicial laws, the Old Covenant's moral laws were not pedagogical in nature. They were meant to permanently protect God's people from sin. That's why, even though Jesus declared all foods clean, he did not declare all sexual relationships to be clean, and so he affirmed the Mosaic Law's prohibition on adultery (Matt 5:27–28). Or, to cite another example, even though Paul said circumcision was not necessary for and could even hinder one's salvation, he also said that the man in 1 Corinthians 5 who was having sex with his stepmother (a violation of Leviticus 18:8 and Deuteronomy 22:30) should be cast out of the community.

These unchanging moral laws related to sinful sexual behavior (along with laws related to other evils, such as idolatry or murder) are as permanent as my mother's ban on Drano martinis. I might have grown up enough to cross a busy street without help, but there's no age that would protect me from drinking poison. Likewise, God's people no longer needed the ceremonial laws in order to be holy, but there is no circumstance in which sins such as murder and fornication could ever be appropriate. Even most die-hard critics of the Bible admit that the Old Testament's prohibitions on child sacrifice, bestiality, and incest are still worth following.

14. Why doesn't the Bible condemn slavery?

Slavery was a universal institution in the ancient world that, like poverty and war, had no place in God's ultimate plan for humanity. God's desire was that there would be no poverty (Deut. 15:4), and that his people would transform their weapons of war into agricultural tools and never fight again (Isa. 2:4). However, in order to overcome the effects of sin and hardened hearts, God progressively revealed himself to his people and tolerated certain evils that their hard hearts embraced. These evils were not meant to last forever, which is why God's word contained regulations designed to reduce and eventually eliminate them.

For example, the Old Testament does not instruct the Israelites to treat slaves in the same way one would treat an animal or a chair. If a master seriously injured a slave by knocking out a tooth or an eye, he had to set the slave free (Exod. 21:26–27). Slaves could not work on the Sabbath (Exod. 20:10), and were allowed to participate in religious festivals, a freedom that was unheard of elsewhere in the ancient world (Exod. 12:44). Slaves could marry free persons (1 Chron. 2:34–35), own property, and even own other slaves (2 Sam. 19:17). If an ox killed a slave, then the ox would be stoned, which was the same punishment that was administered for the killing of a free person (Exod. 21:28–36). Fugitive slaves from other nations could not be returned to their masters and were allowed to live without oppression in the land of Israel (Deut. 23:15–16).

In many respects, Israel's slave laws were superior to those in the surrounding cultures. The Code of Hammurabi, for example, prescribed the death penalty for sheltering fugitive slaves and only required a modest fine for the crime of injuring someone else's slave.[60] The code did not prescribe a punishment for mistreating one's own slave. According to Old Testament scholar C.J. Wright: "No other ancient Near Eastern law has been found that holds a master to account for the treatment of his own slaves (as distinct from injury done to the slave of another master), and the otherwise universal law regarding runaway slaves was that they must be sent back, with severe penalties for those who failed to comply."[61]

This incremental approach to eliminating slavery could be compared to the current incremental approach many pro-life advocates take toward eliminating abortion in the United States. In the same way, the authors of the Old Testament passed laws that helped remove some of the worst abuses that were present in ancient Mesopotamian slavery and set the stage for God's people to eventually reject the institution of slavery in its entirety. By the time of the New Testament, St. Paul exhorted slaves to acquire their freedom:

> Every one should remain in the state in which he was called. Were you a slave when called? Never mind. But if you can gain your freedom, avail yourself of the opportunity. For he who was called in the Lord as a slave is a freedman of the Lord. Likewise he who was free when called is a slave of Christ. You were bought with a price; do not become slaves of men. So, brethren, in whatever state each was called, there let him remain with God (1 Cor. 7:20–24).

Being enslaved to men was an imperfect part of this life that had no place in the kingdom of God. In that kingdom, everyone, regardless of socioeconomic background, is a slave of Christ, our true Lord and master. That's why in Galatians 3:28 Paul says, "There is neither Jew nor Greek, there is neither slave nor free, there is neither male nor female; for you are all one in Christ Jesus." This was a revolutionary idea, given that Roman intellectuals, while lamenting some aspects of slavery, generally held slaves to be of lesser worth than free men.[62] Slaves in the early Church, however, were not stigmatized and some, like Pius I (140–155) and Callixtus I (218–223), even held the office of pope.

It's important to remember that just because the Bible regulates a practice, even an evil one, that doesn't mean God recommends that practice. Instead, God progressively revealed his revelation to hard-hearted people who had to be incrementally led away from the evils of this world. Slavery was a universal feature of ancient economies just as credit is a universal feature of today's economies. God's people could not end slavery outright but they did promote the humane treatment of slaves as well as the intrinsic dignity of all people, which led to slavery being abolished by later Christians.

15. Why does God seem different in the Old Testament compared with the New?

Old Testament professor David Lamb tells us in his book *God Behaving Badly* that he asks his students this question: "Why does the wrathful God of the New Testament seem so different from the loving god of the Old Testament?"[63]

Does Lamb's question seem backward? Don't you hear most people say that they like the God of the New Testament, who preaches love, but they hate the "fire and brimstone" God of the Old Testament? This attitude isn't new and can be traced all the way back to the second-century heretic Marcion of Sinope.

Marcion was at one time a faithful Christian who lavishly supported the Church at Rome with profits from his shipbuilding business.[64] But his donations were returned to him after he was excommunicated for advocating heresy. Marcion believed that there were actually two gods: the inferior god of the Old Testament, who directly created the material world, and the superior god of the New Testament, who created everything, including the god of the Old Testament.[65] Marcion also said the only books of the Bible that were inspired were those that advocated the worship of the superior god, which ended up including only Luke's Gospel and some of Paul's writings. The rest of the New Testament, as well as the entirety of the Old Testament, was declared to be uninspired rubbish.

Fortunately, Marcion's efforts to rewrite Scripture failed, and the councils of Hippo and Carthage reaffirmed the canonical status of all the books we recognize today as being part of the Bible. But Marcion's challenge still exists for many. Why does the God of the Old Testament seem so different from the God of the New Testament? It turns out that this question usually betrays a selective remembering of the Bible. Consider the following two passages:

- "By your hard and impenitent heart you are storing up wrath for yourself on the day of wrath when God's righteous judgment will be revealed."

- "The Lord has called you like a wife forsaken and grieved in spirit, like a wife of youth when she is cast off, says your God. For a brief moment I forsook you, but with great compassion I will gather you."

The first passage is not one of God's decrees in the Old Testament but a judgment given by the apostle Paul in Romans 2:5. The second passage comes not from a pastoral letter in the New Testament but from Isaiah 54:6–7. Overall, the idea of eternal damnation is only hinted at in the Old Testament (e.g., Dan. 12:2) but is made explicit in the New Testament's teachings about hell. Jesus even said, "If your eye causes you to sin, pluck it out; it is better for you to enter the kingdom of God with one eye than with two eyes to be thrown into hell, where their worm does not die, and the fire is not quenched" (Mark 9:47–48). Professor Lamb's question no longer seems so farfetched.

And so it is incorrect to say that the Old Testaments portrait of God radically differs from the New Testament portrait. That would be like comparing a couple's parenting of a newborn with their parenting of that same child twenty years later, then saying that the difference proves the child had two different sets of parents! Instead, just as a parent treats a young child differently than an older one, God gave a different revelation to the Israelites, who were struggling in a fierce polytheistic culture, from the one he gave to second-temple Jews living under Roman occupation.

Pope St. John Paul II, decrying the "ignorance of the deep ties linking the New Testament to the Old," said of this contemporary resurgence of Marcionism,

To deprive Christ of his relationship with the Old Testament is therefore to detach him from his roots and to empty his mystery of all meaning. Indeed, to be meaningful, the Incarnation had to be rooted in centuries of preparation. Christ would otherwise have been like a meteor that falls by chance to the earth and is devoid of any connection with human history.[66]

16. Why does God callously strike people down in the Bible, like when he sent two bears to kill forty-two little boys just because they made fun of his prophet?

First, God never intended for us to die, and he endowed our first parents with special graces that would have allowed them to live indefinitely.[67] But after they sinned, those graces were lost and could no longer be passed on to their descendants. This is why the penalty for sin is death (Rom. 6:23). Now that we live in a fallen world God allows us to live for a while to come to know him and share his love with others, but throughout our lives we must remember that life is a gift from God. This means God is allowed to take back that gift whenever he wants to. It belongs to him.

Consider Job who, after learning that his children had been killed in a natural disaster, said, "Naked I came from my mother's womb, and naked shall I return; the Lord gave, and the Lord has taken away;

blessed be the name of the Lord" (Job 1:21). None of us did anything to earn our lives, and so we have no basis for saying God wrongs us by taking away the lives he gave us.

But many people still cringe at stories that seem to depict God cruelly taking life for no good reason. For example, after Elijah was assumed into heaven, the prophet Elisha continued Elijah's ministry. 2 Kings 2:23–25 describes an event that disturbs many people:

> [Elisha] went up from there [Jericho] to Bethel; and while he was going up on the way, some small boys came out of the city and jeered at him, saying, "Go up, you baldhead! Go up, you baldhead!" And he turned around, and when he saw them, he cursed them in the name of the Lord. And two she-bears came out of the woods and tore forty-two of the boys. From there he went on to Mount Carmel, and thence he returned to Samaria.

Notice that Elisha cursed the boys and then the bears attacked them. Just because one event happened after another does not mean the two events have a causal relationship. God may have known the bear attack was imminent and simply chosen not to stop it. It may even be the case that this story comes from a past recollection of a tragedy that provided a basis for a narrative that is not in the historical genre. But let's suppose that the bears were actually sent by God to attack the boys. Are there elements in the text that modern readers may be missing, things that show it isn't as harsh as they think?

Note that they weren't a couple of small children harmlessly teasing Elisha; they were a large, threatening group of young men. The Hebrew words often translated as "small boys" is *hunearim qetannim*. *Qetannim* comes from *qatan* and means "small, young, least"; it doesn't specifically designate the boys' ages. *Hunearim* is derived from the Hebrew *na'ar*, which means "boy," "lad," or "youth." In Scripture this word is predominantly used of young men who are over the age of twelve, such as Isaac (Gen. 22:12) and Joseph (Gen. 37:2).

Now, imagine if over forty teenage boys started making fun of you as you walked by yourself across a desolate area. You might become nervous, knowing that such a large group could cause you serious harm. In some third-world countries, gangs of children as young as eleven commonly rob and even kill people in broad daylight.[68] According to *The Bible Knowledge Commentary*, "That forty-two men were mauled by the two bears suggests that a mass demonstration had been organized against God and Elisha."[69]

The boy's taunt to "go up" was almost certainly a reference to Elijah's assumption into heaven. It represented a desire for Elisha and his God to "get out of here" and disappear in a similar way. The boy's taunts about his baldness may have been directed not at his mere appearance but toward his decision to serve the God of Israel (some prophets shaved their heads). It also could have been an epithet on par with calling someone an "idiot" regardless of his actual intelligence. Either way, the boys demonstrated profound lack of respect both for God and the prophets he sent. Rachelle Gilmour, in her study of the Elisha narratives, wrote: "It is no longer just an insult to Elisha, it is an insult to the Lord, and the bears appear only after a curse in his name."

Modern people balk at the violence and loss of life in biblical stories like this one, but what is usually absent from their criticisms is a concern about the sins these individuals and groups were guilty of committing. If we recognize that avoiding sin and seeking God with our heart, mind, and strength is what our focus in life should be, then we can understand why gruesome stories that treat sin with a heavy hand are included in Scripture. They serve as warnings not to follow the path that leads to death but to follow the path that leads to eternal life.

17. How could God command the Israelites to kill innocent women and children?

For many people this is the most difficult problem they encounter in Scripture—passages that seem to record God ordering human beings to kill other innocent human beings. One example would be 1 Samuel 15:3, where God tells King Saul to "go and strike Amalek [a tribe that constantly fought with Israel], and utterly destroy all that they have; do not spare them, but kill both man and woman, infant and suckling, ox and sheep, camel and donkey."

What could explain such a harsh command?

In the book of Genesis, God told Abraham that he would "be buried in a good old age. And they [Abraham's descendants] shall come back here [to the land of Canaan] in the fourth generation; for the iniquity of the Amorites is not yet complete" (Gen. 15:15–16). The Amorites were a group of mountain-dwelling Canaanites, but the iniquity God referred to was also present in the other Canaanites who inhabited the land. This includes worship of deities that committed murder, incest, and even bestiality. Fr. Raymond Brown wrote:

> Canaanite worship was socially destructive. Its religious acts were pornographic and sick, seriously damaging to children, creating early impressions of deities with no interest in moral behavior. It tried to dignify, by the use of religious labels, depraved acts of bestiality and corruption. It had a low estimate of human life. It suggested that anything was permissible, promiscuity, murder, or anything else, in order to guarantee a good crop at harvest. It ignored the highest values both in the family and in the wider community—love, loyalty, purity, peace and

security—and encouraged the view that all these things were inferior to material prosperity, physical satisfaction, and human pleasure. A society where those things matter most is self-destructive.[70]

God was committed to shepherding a chosen people from which would come the Messiah, who would atone for the sins of all people, including the Canaanites. But this chosen people had to be protected from idolatry and other sins that would cause them to turn away from the one, true God. Since the habitable areas around God's chosen people were already occupied, God had to forcibly remove some people from these lands so that his chosen people could prosper and eventually bring their knowledge of him to the entire world.

Remember also that God has the right to take any human being's life, regardless of age or moral character. If God has the right to end our lives with a plague or a bolt of lightning, then he has the right to end our lives through the use of human mediators. In the case of the Canaanites, this took the form of the Israelite soldiers. St. Thomas Aquinas put it this way:

All men alike, both guilty and innocent, die the death of nature: which death of nature is inflicted by the power of God on account of original sin, according to 1 Samuel 2:6: "The Lord killeth and maketh alive." Consequently, by the command of

God, death can be inflicted on any man, guilty or innocent, without any injustice whatever.[71]

It could also be the case that the language used in these texts is exaggerated, nonliteral "warfare rhetoric." This kind of language is akin to saying that your favorite sports team "destroyed" or "massacred" its opponents. Phrases such as "all were struck down with the edge of the sword," repeated over and over again in these passages, are typical of the hyperbole used in ancient battle accounts. For example, the Egyptian Merneptah Stele says that Israel was "laid waste and his seed is not," even though the nation of Israel continued to exist for several centuries after the stele was erected.

Other ancient Syrian and Egyptian texts describe how opposing armies were "completely destroyed," even instantaneously, but those same texts also refer to the continued existence of the supposedly decimated forces.[72] We see something similar in the Bible, where the book of Judges records the Israelites' destroying only the Canaanite idols (Judg. 6:25–27)—not the people as a whole, as the book of Joshua seems to describe. Judges 1:28 even says, "When Israel grew strong, they put the Canaanites to forced labor, but did not utterly drive them out." This stands in contrast to Joshua's hyperbolic description of the Canaanites being "utterly destroyed" (Jos. 6:21, 11:21).

Granted, there would still have been civilian casualties when Israel fought the Canaanites, just as there are in modern wars, but those noncombatants would not have been Israel's main targets, nor was it the case that Israel "wiped out" these peoples. Joshua 6:21's reference to the slaughter of "men and women" (in Hebrew "from man (and) unto woman") and "young and old" may involve expressions equivalent to "everyone" or "all the people." They may not literally refer to the killing of non-combatant women and children. In fact, Richard Hess has argued that Jericho and many other conquered cities described in the book of Joshua were primarily military forts and so there would have been few civilian casualties. Most noncombatants would have resided in the countryside surrounding the fort and fled when the battle began.[73]

In sum, the Church has not definitively taught how we should interpret these kinds of Scripture passages. They might be literal accounts of the past that challenge our moral intuitions, or they might be nonliteral accounts that demand an understanding of ancient genres and literary forms. Or they may be a blend of the literal and the nonliteral. The fact that these texts are challenging does not mean that they are intractable; as we've seen, there are several plausible ways to explain them without sacrificing God's goodness or the inerrancy of his sacred word.

18. Was the Bible's text corrupted when it was copied in the early Church?

There currently exist over 5,500 copies of New Testament manuscripts written in Greek, as well as 15,000 manuscripts written in other languages, including Latin, Coptic, and Syriac. Fifty of the Greek manuscripts can be dated to within 250 years of the original copies. The first complete copy of the New Testament, called Codex Sinaiticus (because it was discovered in a monastery at the foot of Mount Sinai), can be dated to within 300 years of the original documents.

Now, compare this with Homer's *Iliad*, which was written in the eighth century B.C. Although a few fragments of the *Iliad* can be dated to within 500 years of Homer, the oldest complete copy of the *Iliad* (a manuscript scholars refer to as Venetus A) was written in the tenth century A.D., or 1,800 years later! Biblical scholar F.F. Bruce put it bluntly: "There is no body of ancient literature in the world which enjoys such a wealth of good textual attestation as the New Testament."[74]

The reason we have so many copies of the New Testament is that as new Church communities sprang up in Europe and Asia, each wanted one for public liturgies as well as for private reading. During this time, Christianity was illegal within the Roman Empire, so Christians who copied the New Testament, or scribes, endured monotonous hours of writing by hand and risked painful deaths just so others could have a copy of Scripture. As modern readers, we should feel very spoiled every time we encounter a free Bible in a hotel room or on the Internet.

Although some of these copies have been lost, many others survived due in large part to the idea that scribal copying was a way to glorify God. The products of this divine service were then revered and protected for centuries. In the sixth century, the monk Cassiodorus, who was a contemporary of St. Benedict, said, "What happy application, what praiseworthy industry, to preach unto men by means of the hand, to untie the tongue by means of the fingers, to bring quiet salvation to mortals, and to fight the devil's insidious wiles with pen and ink!"[75]

Along with faithful scribes, we also have the testimony of faithful Church Fathers, who glorified God by teaching and commenting on the Bible. Even though the Bible manuscripts they consulted no longer exist, they have survived through quotations in the Fathers' commentaries on Scripture. Bart Ehrman, a critic who often claims that the Bible has been hopelessly corrupted, even admitted that this is a resource for textual critics: "so extensive are these citations that if all other sources for our knowledge of the text of the New Testament were destroyed, they would be sufficient alone *for the reconstruction of practically the entire New Testament.*"[76]

The huge number of ancient manuscripts as well as quotations in the writings of the Church Fathers helps disprove a common conspiracy about the Bible. Popular novels such as *The Da Vinci Code* sometimes assert that the Church hid the "truth" about Jesus by destroying all the early copies of the Gospels and replacing them with ones that better fit their man-made doctrines. But the problem with this theory is that no one was ever in a position to gather up *all* the manuscripts and replace or destroy them.

The fact that we've discovered only fifty manu-scripts from the first few centuries implies that there were hundreds or even thousands more in circulation at the time that, like most manuscripts in the ancient world, were later lost. Moreover, Christians who had heard the traditional readings of Scripture their entire lives would have vigorously challenged any later group that tried to change the biblical text. St. Augustine once told St. Jerome that the people of Tripoli rioted in the streets because Jerome's new translation of the book of Jonah was so unfamiliar to them.[77] Imagine what these people would do if a completely new story about Christ were presented to them!

The sheer number of manuscripts that existed, spread over hundreds of thousands of square miles in an area hostile to Christian activity, kept in the custody of Christians who opposed the slightest change to the text, makes any claim that a conspiracy in the early Church to alter the Bible tenable only in the realm of fiction.

19. Which translation of the Bible is the best?

The original manuscripts of the Bible were not written in English. Rather, the New Testament was written in ancient Greek and the Old Testament in ancient Hebrew, along with some Aramaic and Greek (the Old Testament was later translated into the Greek Septuagint). As time went on, the Church in the West translated these texts into Latin as well as popular languages such as German, French, and English. Today, the entire Bible has been translated into over 500 languages.

Even within one language there are usually many different translations, each with its own renderings of the passages found in the original languages. How can this be? The art of translation is not as simple as taking a word in one language and then using a dictionary to find the equivalent word in another language. Translators have different opinions about how words and phrases in a text should be reproduced into another language that has a different vocabulary, different rules of grammar, and different cultural attitudes than the language of the text being translated.

A translator's basic approach tends to fall into one of two kinds. One approach is called *formal equivalence*, and it strives to communicate, as literally as possible, translations of the original words the author used. The most formally equivalent translations of Scripture would be interlinear bibles, which simply replace the original words in the biblical text with their modern counterparts. Using an interlinear translation, John 3:16 reads like this: "Thus indeed loved God the world that the Son the only-begotten he gave that everyone believing in him not should perish but might have life."

As you can see, interlinear translations sound stilted and can be confusing because they take words that made sense in one language and blindly transfer them into another language without considering that language's grammar. Most other formally equivalent translations change the order and kinds of words that are used in order to help modern audiences understand the author's original meaning. The Revised Standard Version (RSV), which tends to be formally equivalent in its translation, renders John 3:16 in this way: "For God so loved the world that he gave his only Son, that whoever believes in him should not perish but have eternal life."

The other approach to translation is *dynamic equivalence*, which strives to communicate the original *idea* the author intended to convey even if it does not use his original words. This can be seen in translations that render the Greek word *dikaiosis* "considered righteous" instead of the traditional term "justified," as in James 2:24, "a man is justified by works and not by faith alone."

Some dynamic-equivalence translations play very loose with the original-language text. *The Message* is an extreme example of this approach, especially since it is not technically a translation of the Bible, but more of a paraphrase that summarizes what the translator, in this case Eugene H. Peterson, thinks the Bible means or what he thinks Jesus would say to people today. For example, in the RSV Matthew 6:11 reads, "Give us this day our daily bread" but *The Message* renders it, "Keep us alive with three square meals." Likewise, *The Message* translates John 3:16 in this way: "This is how much God loved the world: He gave his Son, his one and only Son. And this is why: so that no one need be destroyed; by believing in him, anyone can have a whole and lasting life."

Dynamically equivalent and paraphrased translations may be easier for a modern person to understand, but there is a danger that the reader will encounter the interpretations of the translator more than the words of the sacred author. This can lead to faulty interpretations of the text. For example, in John 3:16, the Greek phrase *zoen aionion* literally means "life eternal" or "eternal life." *The Message*'s translation, "whole and lasting life," could cause readers to think faith in God's son will make them live for a long time, but not forever.

Sometimes a translator's theology will even cause him to mistranslate a text in order to justify his beliefs. This is evident in the *New World Translation* of the Bible, which Jehovah's Witnesses use. In this Bible the first verse of John's Gospel does not say, as it does in the RSV, "In the beginning was the Word, and the Word was with God, and the Word was God" It instead says, "In the beginning was the Word, and the Word was with God, and the Word was *a* god." Jehovah's Witnesses deny the divinity of Christ and think he is just "a god" or a creation of the one almighty God Jehovah.[78]

Although Catholics should be wary of non-Catholic translations of Scripture (especially since they usually lack the deuterocanonical books), there is no single translation of the Bible that all Christians must accept to the exclusion of others. An audience of people at Mass may appreciate a more dynamically equivalent translation of Scripture, such as the New American Bible (NAB), that refrains from using complex or out-dated words that could obscure the author's meaning. A serious Scripture scholar, on the other hand, would prefer a formally equivalent translation, such as the RSV, that uses words that best convey what the sacred author was trying to say in his own language.

The best-known translations for Catholics include the RSV (Catholic Edition), the NAB that we hear at Mass, and the Douay-Rheims, which is an English translation of the Latin Bible translated by St. Jerome, called the Vulgate. What's the best translation for you? The one you will read!

20. How can I develop a better devotion to Scripture?

The most effective way you can develop a devotion to Scripture is to start reading Scripture. It's really that simple. However, as we've seen, the Bible is a complex and lengthy collection of books translated from languages and cultural contexts with which most people are not familiar. As a result, it may not be wise to read the books of the Bible in sequential order beginning with Genesis and ending with Revelation.

Instead, try an order recommended in something like Jeff Cavins's *Bible Timeline*, or start with the Gospels and then read the New Testament letters. The *Ignatius Catholic Study Bible* is a great resource for personal Bible study and, if you're pressed for time, try listening to something like the *Truth and Life Audio Bible*. Along with becoming familiar with Scripture through reading or listening to it, you should try some of these ways to cultivate a devotion to God's word:

- *Attend daily Mass.* Catholics who attend daily Mass will hear a large portion of the Bible read to them over the course of three years. They also have the benefit of meditating on Scripture in the context of the liturgy and the reception of the sacrament of the Eucharist.

- *Pray a scriptural rosary.* They contain the same mysteries as the regular rosary, but also include Scripture verses on each mystery for meditation.

- *Read a reliable commentary.* Commentaries help readers understand details about a passage's original language, its cultural context and literary context, and other elements that might be missed in a casual reading. Along with Scott Hahn and Curtis Mitch's *Ignatius Catholic Study Bible* I recommend the *Navarre Study Bible* and the *Catholic Commentary on Holy Scripture.*

- *Join a Bible study.* Popular Catholic Bible studies include *Little Rock Scripture Study* and *Unlocking the Mystery of the Bible.* You can even take part in specialized studies that relate the Bible to the Catholic Faith, such as Edward Sri's *A Biblical Walk Through the Mass.*

- *Pray the* lectio divina. Rooted in Benedictine spirituality, this approach doesn't study Scripture but allows a person to immerse himself in it through a four-step process of reading, meditating, praying, and contemplating.

Finally, if you want to learn how to defend the inspiration and inerrancy of God's word, as well as how it properly relates to the Church and Sacred Tradition, then I recommend the following books, which I have labeled as being either for beginners (B), intermediate study (I), or advanced study (A) of a subject:

- *20 Answers: Scripture and Tradition* by Jim Blackburn (B)

- *Beginning Apologetics 7: How to Read the Bible* by Fr. Frank Chacon and Jim Burnham (B)

- *The Bible Compass: A Catholic's Guide to Navigating the Scriptures* by Edward Sri (B)

- *The Book of Acts in the Setting of Hellenistic History* by Colin Hemer (A)

- *The Case for the Deuterocanon: Evidence and Arguments* by Gary Michuta (I)

- *Free from All Error* by Fr. William Most (I)

- *Hard Sayings: A Catholic Approach to Answering Bible Difficulties* by Trent Horn (I)

- *The Historical Reliability of the Gospels* by Craig Blomberg (I)

- *The Historical Reliability of John's Gospel* by Craig Blomberg (I)

- *Jesus and the Eyewitnesses: The Gospels as Eyewitness Testimony* by Richard Bauckham (I)

- *The Meaning of Tradition* by Yves Conger (I)

- *On the Reliability of the Old Testament* by K.A. Kitchen (I)

About the Author

Trent Horn is an apologist and speaker for Catholic Answers. He specializes in pro-life issues as well as outreach to atheists and agnostics. He holds a master's degree in theology from Franciscan University of Steubenville. His most recent book, *Hard Sayings: A Catholic Approach to Bible Difficulties*, is published by Catholic Answers Press.

Endnotes

1 *Providentissimus Deus*, 10.

2 *Verbum Domini*, 7, quoting CCC 108.

3 Jasper James Ray, *God Wrote Only One Bible* (Junction City, KS: The Eye Opener Publishers, 1955), 118.

4 The Pontifical Biblical Commission, *The Interpretation of the Bible in the Church* (Washington, DC: USCCB Publishing, 1993), 19.

5 *Dei Verbum*, 11.

6 *Dei Verbum*, 13.

7 "Address of Pope John Paul II to Pontifical Biblical Commission," April 23, 1993, in *The Scripture Documents: An Anthology of Official Catholic Teachings*, ed. Dean P. Bechard (Collegeville, MN: The Order of Saint Benedict, 2002), 174.

8 *Dei Verbum*, 11.

9 *Divino Afflante Spiritu*, 35–36.

10 Pontifical Biblical Commission, *The Inspiration and Truth of Sacred Scripture*, (Collegeville, MN: Liturgical Press, 2014) 120.

11 *Dei Verbum*, 12.

12 *Dei Verbum*, 10. Pope Benedict XVI also said, "The Holy Spirit, who gives life to the Church, enables us to interpret the scriptures authoritatively. The Bible is the Church's book, and its essential place in the Church's life gives rise to its genuine interpretation" (*Verbum Domini*, 29).

13 Patrick Madrid, "Sola Scriptura: A Blueprint for Anarchy," in *Not by Scripture Alone: A Catholic Critique of the Protestant Doctrine of Sola Scriptura,* ed. Robert Sungenis (Santa Barbara, CA: Queenship Publishing, 1997).

14 St. Irenaeus, *Against Heresies,* 1:10:2, 3:4:1.

15 St. Vincent of Lerins, *Commonitory,* 2.5.

16 Eusebius, *Church History*, 4:23:11.

17 R.C. Sproul, *What Is Reformed Theology? Understanding the Basics* (Grand Rapids, MI: Baker Books, 2005), 54.

18 Luther placed James with Jude and Hebrews in the back of the Bible. Luther did not want to reject these books as Scripture, but he also did not want to give them the same authority as other writings in the Bible that he preferred, such as Romans. See Timothy George, *Theology of the Reformers* (Nashville, TN: Broadman and Holman Publishing, 2013), 84–85.

19 For a defense of the inspiration of the deuterocanonical books, see Gary Michuta, *The Case for the Deuterocanon: Evidence and Arguments* (Livonia, MI: Nikaria Press, 2015).

20 Douglas Wilson, "A Severed Branch," *Credenda Agenda*, vol. 12, issue 1. http://www.credenda.org/archive/issues/12-1thema.php.

21 *Dei Verbum*, 10.

22 Bruce Metzger, *Introduction to the Apocrypha* (New York: Oxford University Press, 1957), 171.

23 See, for example, Steve Ray, "The Council That Wasn't," *This Rock Magazine*, vol. 15, no. 7, September 2004.

24 "[Rabbi] Akiba's repudiation shows that there must have existed a wide acceptance of the Deuterocanon as sacred texts (along with the New Testament) among Jewish Christians *in Judea before* AD 132." Gary Michuta, *The Case for the Deuterocanon: Evidence and Arguments* (Livonia, MI: Nikaria Press, 2015) 62. See 55–65 for a full treatment.

25 For a complete list of Patristic citations and analysis, see Michuta,

The Case for the Deuterocanon, 107–249.

26 J.N.D. Kelly, *Early Christian Doctrines* (New York: HarperCollins, 1978), 55.

27 St. Basil the Great, *Moralia, Regula* LXXX, XXII: PG 31, 867. Cited in *Verbum Domini*, 48.

28 *Providentissimus Deus,* 20.

29 Pontifical Biblical Commission, *The Inspiration and Truth of Sacred Scripture*, 70.

30 *Dei Verbum*, 11.

31 For an in-depth treatment of this issue, see *Letter and Spirit, Vol. 6: For the Sake of Our Salvation: The Truth and Humility of God's Word,* ed. Scott Hahn and David Scott (Steubenville, OH: Emmaus Road Publishing, 2010), especially the entries by Hahn, Pitre, and Fr. Harrison.

32 *Divino Afflante Spiritu*, 1.

33 *Dei Verbum*, 11.

34 *Verbum Domini*, 42.

35 For evidence for the theory of evolution that does not come from authors with an atheistic worldview, see Francis Collins, *The Language of God: A Scientist Presents Evidence for Belief* (New York: Free Press, 2007), and Kenneth Miller, *Finding Darwin's God: A Scientist's Search for Common Ground Between God and Evolution* (New York: Harper Perennial, 2007).

36 St. Augustine, *The Literal Meaning of Genesis*, 1.14.

37 Ibid., 15.29.

38 Alister McGrath, *The Passionate Intellect: Christian Faith and the Discipleship of the Mind* (Downers Grove, IL: InterVarsity Press, 2010), 140.

39 *Humani Generis*, 38.

40 Pope John Paul II, General Audience, November 7, 1979, www.vatican.va/holy_father/john_paul_ii/audiences/catechesis_genesis/documents/hf_jp-ii_aud_19791107_en.html.

41 See canons 1–5 of the First Vatican Council (1870), and Pope Pius XII's encyclical *Humani Generis* (1950).

42 "The name Israel is followed by a different sign: 'man + woman + three strokes,' which refers to peoples in contrast to nation-states or their capitals—in other words, to an ethnic group." William G. Dever, *Who Were the Early Israelites and Where Did They Come From?* (Grand Rapids, MI: Wm. B. Eerdmans), 202.

43 "The Light of Revelation in the Old Testament," Wednesday Audience, May 8, 1985.

44 Israel Finkelstein and Avi Perevolotsky, "Processes of Sedentarization and Nomadization in the History of Sinai and the Negev," *Bulletin of the American Schools of Oriental Research,* no. 279 (August 1990): 67–88. Cited in James K. Hoffmeier, *Ancient Israel in Sinai: The Evidence for the Authenticity of the Wilderness Tradition* (New York: Oxford University Press, 2005), 150.

45 For example, an 1882 article in the *British Quarterly Review* says, "In 1857 Professor F.W. Newman, fellow of Balliol College, Oxford, in his *History of the Hebrew Monarchy* [178–79] speaks of the Bible references to the Hittites as 'unhistorical,' and as 'not exhibiting the writer's acquaintance with the times in a very favourable light,' and the Rev. T.K. Cheyne, fellow of the same college, writing on the Hittites, in the *Encyclopaedia Britannica*, last year, treats the Bible statements regarding the Hittites as unhistorical and unworthy of credence." "The Hittites and the Bible," *British Quarterly*

Review (July and October 1882): 54.

46 Horst Klengel, "Problems in Hittite History, Solved and Unsolved," in *Recent Developments in Hittite Archaeology and History: Papers in Memory of Hans G. Guterbock*, ed. K. Aslihan Yener, Harry A. Hoffner, and Simrit Dhesi (Winona Lake, IN: Eisenbrauns, 2002), 101.

47 See the introduction to Tacitu' *Annals* at the Loeb Classical Library online at http://penelope.uchicago.edu/Thayer/E/Roman/Texts/Tacitus/Annals/Introduction.

48 St. Augustine, *Contra Faustum*, XXXIII.6.

49 See, for example, Bart Ehrman, *Jesus: Apocalyptic Prophet of the New Millennium* (New York: Oxford University Press, 1999), 248–250.

50 Brant Pitre, *The Case for Jesus: The Biblical and Historical Evidence for Christ* (New York: Doubleday, 2016), 17.

51 Granted, some may use this argument to try to prove that John's Gospel is a forgery, but the eyewitness details in that text and external sources that corroborate John's authorship make the Fourth Gospel completely different in kind to the forgeries that came centuries later (for more, see Craig Blomberg's book *The Historical Reliability of John's Gospel*).

52 Rob Bell, *Velvet Elvis: Repainting the Christian Faith* (New York: HarperOne, 2005), 124–126.

53 These sources include the *Buddhacharita* by Aśvaghosa and Plutarch's *Life of Alexander*.

54 Justin Martyr, *Dialogue with Trypho*, 65.

55 Karl Keating, *What Catholics Really Believe: Answers to Common Misconceptions About the Faith* (San Francisco: Ignatius Press, 1992), 37–38. Cardinal Ratzinger also said, "It is because faith is

not set before us as a complete and finished system that the Bible contains contradictory texts, or at least ones that stand in tension to each other." Joseph Cardinal Ratzinger and Peter Seewald, *God and the World: Believing and Living in Our Time* (San Francisco: Ignatius Press, 2000), 152.

56 Mark Giszczak, *Light on the Dark Passages of Scripture* (Huntington, IN: Our Sunday Visitor, 2015), 144.

57 *Dei Verbum*, 15. Cited in CCC 122.

58 Mark Giszczak, *Light on the Dark Passages of Scripture*, 40.

59 See also St. Thomas Aquinas, *Summa Theologica*, 1.2.103.3.

60 "If any one receive into his house a runaway male or female slave of the court, or of a freedman, and does not bring it out at the public proclamation of the major domus, the master of the house shall be put to death." Law of Hammurabi 16. Translated by L.W. King. Available online at avalon.law.yale.edu/ancient/hamframe.asp.

61 Christopher J.H. Wright, *Old Testament Ethics for the People of God* (Downers Grove, IL: InterVarsity Press, 2004), 292.

62 One example of this is the philosopher Seneca, who, although he discouraged merciless corporal punishment, compared slaves to valuable property like jewels that one must constantly worry about. According to Joshel, "Seneca sees slaves as inferiors who can never rise above the level of humble friends." Sandra R. Joshel, *Slavery in the Roman World* (New York: Cambridge University Press, 2010), 127.

63 David Lamb, *God Behaving Badly: Is the God of the Old Testament Angry, Sexist, and Racist?* (Downers Grove, IL: InterVarsity Press, 2011), 9.

64 Tertullian refers to Marcion as a shipmaster from Pontus (a nar-

row strip of land on the southern coast of the Black Sea) and says he went "with the two hundred sesterces which he had brought into the church, and, when banished at last to a permanent excommunication, they scattered abroad the poisons of their doctrines." *Prescription Against Heresies*, 30.

65 This idea is rooted in the early heresy of Gnosticism. For a survey of this belief system, see John Arendzen, "Gnosticism," in *The Catholic Encyclopedia,* vol. 6. (New York: Robert Appleton Company, 1909), 20, www.newadvent.org/cathen/06592a.htm.

66 Pope John Paul II, "Old Testament Essential to Know Jesus," Address to the Pontifical Biblical Commission, *L'Osservatore Romano,* April 23, 1997, 2.

67 CCC 402–403, 1008.

68 G.K. Lieten and Talinay Strehl, *Child Street Life: An Inside View of Hazards and Expectations of Street Children in Peru* (New York: Springer, 2015), 22.

69 John F. Walvoord, *The Bible Knowledge Commentary: Old Testament* (Wheaton, IL: Victor Books, 1985), 542.

70 Rachelle Gilmour, *Juxtaposition and the Elisha Cycle* (London: Bloomsbury T&T Clark, 2014), 102.

71 St. Thomas Aquinas, *Summa Theologica*, I–II.94.5.

72 Lawson Younger Jr., *Ancient Conquest Accounts,* 227–228. Cited in Paul Copan and Matt Flanagan, *Did God Really Command Genocide?: Coming to Terms with the Justice of God* (Grand Rapids, MI: Baker Books, 2014), 104.

73 Richard Hess, "The Jericho and Ai of the Book of Joshua," in *Critical Issues in Early Israelite History,* ed. Richard Hess et al. (Winona Lake, IN: Eisenbrauns, 2008), 34.

74 F.F. Bruce, *The Books and the Parchments: How We Got Our English Bible* (Grand Rapids, MI: Fleming H. Revell Co., 1984), 78.

75 Bruce M. Metzger and Bart D. Ehrman, *The Text of the New Testament: Its Transmission, Corruption, and Restoration* (New York: Oxford University Press, 2005), 29.

76 Ibid., 126.

77 "When the bishop of Oea (modern Tripoli) introduced Jerome's recent rendering into his community service, Augustine worriedly related, the congregation nearly rioted. (At issue, perhaps, was the identity of the vine under which the prophet Jonah had rested—a 'gourd' so the traditional version, or an 'ivy' so Jerome; *Letter 75.7,* 22; Jonah 4:6.)" Paula Fredriksen, *Augustine and the Jews: A Christian Defense of Jews and Judaism* (New Haven, CT: Yale University Press, 2010), 289.

78 For more on how to answer these kinds of arguments, see my booklet *20 Answers: Jehovah's Witnesses.*

Become part of the team.
Help support Catholic Answers.

Catholic Answers is an apostolate dedicated to serving Christ by bringing the fullness of Catholic truth to the world. We help good Catholics become better Catholics, bring former Catholics "home," and lead non-Catholics into the fullness of the Faith.

Catholic Answers neither asks for nor receives financial support from any diocese. The majority of its annual income is in the form of donations from individual supporters like you.

To make a donation by phone using your credit card, please speak with one of our customer service representatives at 888-291-8000.

To make a donation by check, please send a check payable to "Catholic Answers" to:

> Catholic Answers
> 2020 Gillespie Way
> El Cajon, CA 92020

To make a donation online, visit **catholic.com**.

TO EXPLAIN & DEFEND THE FAITH

catholic.com